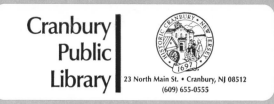

Bug Zone

Bug

Hunters

Barbara Taylor

Chrysalis Education

Distributed in the United States by
Smart Apple Media
1980 Lookout Drive
North Mankato, MN 56003

Copyright © Chrysalis Books PLC 2003

ISBN 1-93233-312-6

Library of Congress Control Number 2003102438

Editorial manager: Joyce Bentley
Assistant editor: Clare Chambers

Project manager and editor: Penny Worms
Designer: Angie Allison
Picture researcher: Jenny Barlow
Consultant: Michael Chinery

Printed in Hong Kong
10 9 8 7 6 5 4 3 2 1

Words in bold can be found in the glossary on page 30.

All reasonable efforts have been made to trace the relevant copyright holders of the images
contained within this book. If we were unable to reach you, please contact Chrysalis Education.

B = bottom; C = center; L = left; R = right; T = top.
Front Cover Montage (main) RSPCA Photolibrary/Wild Images/Andrew Mounter BL M & P Fogden
BCL FLPA/L. West BCR Papilio/Ken Wilson BR RSPCA Photolibrary/D.W Bevan Back Cover L
FLPA/Minden Pictures/M. Moffett R M & P Fogden 1 (see cover) 4 FLPA/Minden Pictures/M. Moffett 5
T Papilio/Michael Maconachie B (see cover) 6 RSPCA Photolibrary/Wild Images/Rupert Barrington 7
(see cover) 8 Papilio/Robert Pickett 9 FLPA/Silvestris 10 FLPA/D. Maslowski 11 T Ecoscene/Williams B
M & P Fogden 12 and 13 FLPA/L. West 14 (see cover) 15 T RSPCA Photolibrary/Wild Images/Carol
Buchanan B M & P Fogden 16 Corbis/Gallo Images/Anthony Bannister 17 Ecoscene/Wayne Lawler 18
(see cover) 19 M & P Fogden 20 Papilio/Ken Wilson 21 FLPA/Minden Pictures/M. Moffett 22 (see
cover) 23 FLPA/B. Casals 24 FLPA/L. West 25 M & P Fogden 26 FLPA/Foto Natura/J van Arkel
27 FLPA/ T. Davidson 28 and 29 M & P Fogden.

Contents

How do bugs hunt?

Jumping **spiders** hunt like tigers—they prowl around and then pounce.

There are three main ways for a **bug** to hunt. Some bugs stalk and chase their **prey**. Others **ambush** their victims by hiding or staying still, ready to grab a meal.

Hanging scorpion flies ambush their prey. They dangle from branches and catch passing bugs with their back legs.

Only about half of all spiders spin webs to catch food. The others hunt or ambush their prey.

A few bug hunters set traps for their prey.

Many spiders spin sticky webs to trap bug meals.

Fast food...slow food

Some of the fastest bug hunters are adult tiger **beetles**. They are very fast runners, zooming along on their long legs.

Tiger beetles have large eyes to see their prey and biting jaws to crunch it up.

Tiger beetles
can zip along at up
to 1.6 mph.
This is nearly as fast
as a person walking
normally.

This ladybug
and its **larvae**
are having a tasty
greenfly meal.

The slowest hunters are probably
ladybugs. They slowly march up
and down plants until they bump
into a group of **greenfly**.

7

In-flight meals and submarine snacks

Robber **flies** grab their prey with their hairy legs as they fly. **Dragonflies** catch food like this too.

Bugs catch prey in the air and under the water as well as on land. Some flying bugs jump from a perch to grab a meal as it flies past. Others catch their prey in flight.

A great diving beetle is such a speedy swimmer that it is able to catch fast-swimming newts.

Underwater hunters need swimming speed or **camouflage** to catch their prey.

Robber flies often catch bees and wasps. The stings don't seem to bother them!

Ultimate ambush

Some bugs use camouflage to play a deadly game of hide-and-seek. They are the same shape and colors as the flowers or leaves around them. They keep still…wait for prey to get close…then they grab!

Look out **grasshopper**, there's a praying mantis behind you!

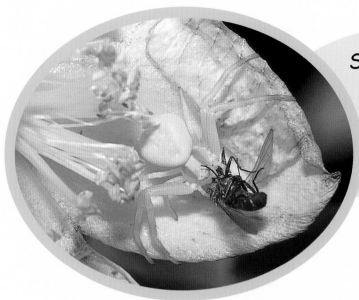

Some crab spiders can even change color to match different flowers.

Mantises can turn their heads right round, so they can spot prey anywhere.

Flower **mantises** and crab spiders look like the flowers in which they hide.

Any bug landing on this flower is quickly trapped by the mantis.

Stalking spiders

The green lynx spider uses its long legs to leap from leaf to leaf after prey.

Some hunting spiders use camouflage and surprise to catch their prey. Others use speed and strength to overcome their victims.

There are many different kinds of hunting spiders, from the big, hairy tarantulas to the tiny jumping spiders.

Lynx spiders can jump nearly an inch into the air to grab a flying insect.

Wolf spiders chase their prey. This pirate wolf spider lives in boggy places and can even chase **insects** over the water's surface.

Sticky traps

Spiders use **silk** to make their webs. A typical web is like a wheel, made of sticky threads that trap flying or jumping insects.

Spider silk is stretchier than rubber, stickier than Scotch tape, and stronger than material used for bulletproof vests!

Spiders' webs are almost invisible, yet incredibly strong.

An orb web spider wraps its prey into a silk parcel to stop it from escaping.

When something is trapped in its web, a spider moves in for the kill, walking along non-sticky threads.

The net-casting spider throws a strong, stretchy net over its prey.

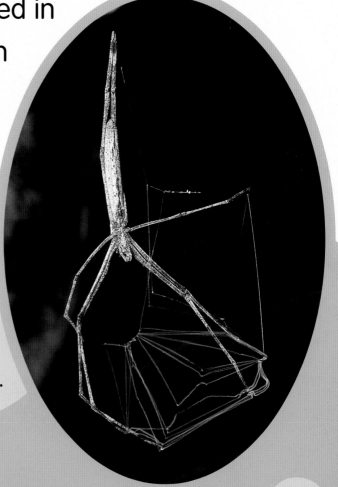

Hidden traps

Trapdoor spiders wait inside burrows that have a trapdoor made of silk and soil. When prey is passing, the spider opens its door and grabs its meal.

Trapdoor spiders know when prey is near because they set up silk trip-wires. When creatures trip over the silk, the spiders feel the movements.

Antlion larvae have strong **pincer** jaws to grab and kill their prey.

Some antlion larvae dig a steep pit in sand. They lie at the bottom of the pit, waiting for **ants** and other bugs to fall in.

Hungry antlion larvae flick sand at ants trying to escape up the pit walls to make them fall back down.

17

How do bugs kill?

A mantis bites deeply into its victims with its powerful jaws.

Mantises are **cannibals**—they eat other mantises, including their mates!

Once a bug has caught its prey, it may start eating it alive. Mantises and ladybugs do this.

If the prey struggles or fights back,
it may escape or injure the hunter.
So some bugs use deadly poison
to **paralyze** or kill their prey.

Can you see the sharp **fangs** on this spider? Spiders use these fangs to inject poison into their prey.

Giant jaws

Many beetles are fierce meat-eaters. Most beetles seize their victims in their powerful jaws and then crush or crunch them up to kill them.

This ground beetle is a fast runner so that it can chase after prey.

Can you see the huge jaws on its head?

The sharp, biting jaws of a beetle
work like a pair of scissors.

The boat-backed ground
beetle has a narrow head and
long, narrow jaws to help it
reach inside a snail's shell and
seize the juicy snail inside.

Male stag
beetles have huge
jaws but they are
used for fighting
not for eating.

Clasping claws, deadly jaws

A scorpion has small but strong jaws to pull food to pieces and crush it to a soft pulp.

Just like cats, some bugs use their claws to capture their prey. **Scorpions** have huge pincers to hold their prey with a tight grip.

Great diving beetle larvae catch prey by stabbing it with their big, curved jaws. They pump juices into their prey and then suck up the insides.

Some scorpions can survive for more than a year without eating!

Can you see the curved jaws on this diving beetle larva?

Poison swords

Assassin means killer, so it is no surprise that assassin bugs are fierce hunters. They have sword-like beaks, through which they inject poison.

Assassin bugs have long legs to chase after prey. Some use their strong, spiny front legs to grab their victims.

An assassin bug may take days to eat a large victim, such as this grasshopper.

The poison turns the insides of the prey into mushy soup so the bug can suck its victim dry.

Some assassin bugs dip their legs into sticky tree resin. This makes it easier to trap their prey before they kill it.

Kids' meals

Young bugs are called larvae or **nymphs**. They are not cared for by adult bugs, so they have to hunt and kill for themselves.

Damselfly nymphs shoot out a long lower lip with claws on the end to capture prey.

The nymphs of dragonflies and **damselflies** live and hunt underwater. When they become adults, they live above water and eat land or air creatures.

Some green **lacewing** larvae disguise themselves as pieces of garbage, using the skins of their victims.

This lacewing larva is eating a greenfly, which it has killed with its jaws.

Group attack

Most bugs hunt alone, but tropical driver and army ants hunt in groups. Together they can attack creatures as large as farm animals.

Army and driver ants do not have leaders. They take turns.

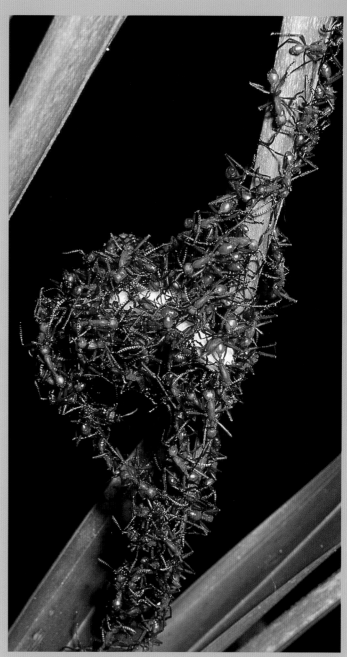

Army ants hunt in huge groups. These are carrying a wasp larva.

Instead of marching around looking for food, fungus gnat larvae from New Zealand hang from cave ceilings and glow in the dark.

Bugs attracted to the lights become caught on sticky strands dangling below the larvae. The captured prey is hauled up and eaten!

Words to remember

ant A small insect that lives with other ants in a large group called a colony.

ambush To hide and wait, ready to attack.

beetle An insect with tough front wings that cover most of its body like a case.

bug A true bug is a type of insect with a stabbing beak. The word "bug" is now used to mean any type of minibeast.

camouflage Colors or patterns that blend in with the background.

cannibal An animal that eats others of its own kind.

damselfly A meat-eating insect like a dragonfly, but smaller and slower in flight. It rests with its wings together.

dragonfly A large, meat-eating insect that flies well and rests with its wings spread out.

fangs Sharp, pointed mouthparts used to inject poison into prey or enemies.

fly A flying insect with only two wings.

grasshopper A jumping insect with long, powerful back legs. It usually has wings, too.

greenfly Small, green bugs.

insect A minibeast with three parts to its body and six legs. Most insects can fly.

lacewing A small, delicate insect with two pairs of flimsy wings covered in a network of fine veins, like lace.

ladybug A type of small beetle, usually red with black spots.

larva A young insect, such as a caterpillar, that looks different from its parents. A larva is usually the feeding and growing stage in the life cycle. The word for more than one larva is larvae.

mantis A meat-eating insect with large, spiky front legs and a long neck.

nymph A young insect that looks like its parents but is smaller and cannot fly.

paralyze To make something unable to move.

pincers Large claws that grip together.

prey An animal that is killed or eaten by another animal.

scorpion A minibeast (not an insect) with two big claws and a powerful sting in its tail.

silk A fine, strong fiber produced by spiders and some insects and used to make webs and cocoons.

spider A minibeast (not an insect) with eight legs, two parts to its body, and two poisonous fangs.

Index